the Loch N
MONSTER

Colin Baxter Photography, Grantown-on-Spey, Scotland

the Loch Ness Monster

Although very few people can actually claim to have seen it, the Loch Ness Monster is probably one of the world's best-known creatures. For reasons that aren't entirely clear, 'Nessie', as she's affectionately known – assuming, of course, the monster is female – has beome a staple element of popular culture in the UK and North America.

Over the years, Nessie has featured regularly in books, films and even in starring roles of many classic television series. And as you travel across Scotland, particularly across the Highlands, the winsome little monster with the tartan tammy smiles back at you from countless postcards, brochures, signs and a raft of souvenirs.

However, it wasn't always so.

Monsters have always had a grip on the popular imagination and as far back as biblical times, have formed a significant body of folklore and legends in all cultures. This was certainly true in Scotland, which has a rich tradition of mythological creatures, several of which inhabit or are directly associated with bodies of water. A number of lochs reputedly boast monsters of their own, such as Morag, the monster believed to inhabit Loch Morar in Lochaber in the western Highlands. Other beasts such as silkies, kelpies, and the *each uisge* or water horse also feature prominently in Highland folk tales. However, unlike the cuddly Nessie depictions of today, these were traditionally malevolent creatures, to be feared and avoided at all costs. The *each uisge*, for example, was a shape-shifting water spirit that often appeared as a handsome horse that would entice the unwary to mount it. When ridden anywhere near to water, the *each uisge's* skin became sticky, and entrapped its rider, who was then carried to the bottom of the loch and devoured – all except the liver, which for some reason was left float to the surface.

Highland culture was rooted firmly in earth, water, fire and air, and tales such as this were perhaps attempts to come to terms with otherwise inexplicable deaths in communities living cheek-by-jowl with the natural world. It's not difficult to picture families gathered round the peat fires in their croft houses recounting tales of strange creatures rising from the dark waters of a loch to snatch and carry off the careless to a watery doom. But like all good fireside tales, the best have perhaps just enough of a grain of truth to make them all the more believable.

The impressive ruins of Urquhart Castle (opposite and below) offer commanding views up and down Loch Ness. Legend has it there are caves beneath the rocky promontory on which the castle stands which allow Nessie to hide from those who attempt to track her down.

A Legend Is Born

Opposite: *a 'Pictish Beast'*
carving from a stone found
at Meigle in Perth and
Kinross. Such carvings were
a common theme on Pictish
stones over a thousand years
ago, and some believe they
represent the mythical
each uisge or even the
Loch Ness Monster itself.

Although the intense public interest in the possibility of a 'monster' inhabiting the depths of Loch Ness is a relatively modern phenomenon, the notion that the loch is home to some large beast has been around for at least 1500 years and probably longer.

Such creatures may be the stuff of legend nowadays but to the pre-Christian tribal societies such as the Picts who occupied the north of Scotland when the Romans invaded, they constituted a very real part of a belief system that was rooted firmly in the landscape, nature and the elements. We know little of the Picts except what we can glean from their large upright 'picture stones'. Amongst the many intricately carved symbols that they featured were depictions of animals and mythological creatures that presumably played an important part in Pictish culture, given the care with which they are carved and the frequency with which they appear. One of these carvings, known to scholars as the Pictish Beast, is clearly an aquatic creature of some kind. with a long snout, flippers and curling tail. Its dragon-like appearance is often taken as proof that the Picts believed in water monsters and links directly to the malevolent water horses and kelpies of Scottish mythology.

It doesn't take too much of a leap of the imagination to understand why people might believe in such things when you see the loch itself: surrounded by steeply rising mountains, it is very deep and very murky due to the high concentrations of peat sediment in the water, with few signs of life below the surface. On dark nights with only the moon reflecting on the rippling surface, it definitely has an otherworldly feel to it.

In fact, the first recorded sighting of the creature in Loch

⇒ THE LOCH ⇒

Loch Ness is an immense body of water. Over 23 miles long and around a mile wide, it forms a dramatic diagonal gash across the Highland landscape, running from Inverness at its north end to Fort Augustus at its south. It sits on the Great Glen geological fault which is still active and capable of generating three or four earthquakes each century that register up to 4 on the Richter Scale. Although Loch Lomond boasts a larger surface area, Loch Ness holds the greatest volume of water of any loch in Scotland. In fact, it contains more water than all the lakes in England and Wales put together. This is because of the loch's great depth, which averages around 180 m (600 feet) and plunges to over 220 m (750 feet) to the south of Urquhart Castle. It may even be deeper than this because of the thick sediment coating the bottom of the loch: in 1987, a local boat skipper George Edwards, is believed to have recorded its greatest known depth at 248 m (812 feet) – that's twice the height of Edinburgh Castle Rock and surely deep enough to hide a monster!

Ness dates back to the sixth century, and is attributed to no less a figure than St Columba, who is credited with bringing Christianity to Scotland and converting the Picts. According to Columba's biographer, Adamnan, in AD 565 the saint was travelling across the Highlands preaching to the heathen Picts when he came across a local being attacked by a fiercesome beast which had risen up from the depths of the loch as the man was swimming close to the shore. Columba immediately invoked the name of the Almighty, and commanded the monster, 'Thou shalt go no further, nor touch the man; go back with all speed!' Having literally had the fear of God put into it, the creature abandoned its attack and took off at speed back into the loch.

Detailed and dramatic as the account is, few people today give it much credence as a genuine eyewitness account. For one thing, different versions of the story are told where all the details of what happened, and even the location vary. Also, Adamnan was writing Columba's biography in the middle of the 7th century, almost 100 years after his death and while it is a hugely significant and important medieval document, there are clearly a number of question marks over its historical accuracy. In fact, Columba's reputed close encounter at Loch Ness is just one of many extraordinary and miraculous occurrences involving the saint that are described by Adamnan; it's likely these owe less to a concern for any facts and more to the need to have the fledgling Christian faith be seen to triumph over the older prevailing mythology in order to secure converts. Nevertheless, the very fact that Adamnan mentions the creature in the loch points to a long-held belief in such things by the local tribes.

In the centuries that followed, other recorded sightings are few but this would not perhaps be too unexpected in a Highland Gaelic society where the oral tradition was stronger than the written one and where communications were generally poor. Various sources, all claiming 'official' status of one sort or another, describe a raft of eyewitness accounts from the late 19th and early 20th centuries although there is little if any supporting evidence for these.

It was not until the early 1930s that the Loch Ness Monster was unleashed on a largely unsuspecting world.

the Nessie Phenomenon

While the belief in large creatures lurking in Loch Ness probably existed for almost two millennia, the birth of the Loch Ness Monster phenomenon as we would recognise it today can be dated quite precisely to a sequence of events that began in the spring of 1933.

On April 14th, an Inverness couple, the Mackays, were driving along the recently opened road on the north side of the loch when Mrs Mackay cried out to her husband to draw his attention to a large creature churning up the otherwise tranquil water in the narrows close to Abriachan pier, 'rolling and plunging for fully a minute, its body resembling that of a whale, and the water cascading ... like a simmering cauldron' as she later described it.

Remarkable as this was, such an encounter was not substantially different from previous anecdotal accounts of sightings of a creature in the loch. What marks it out as the starting point of the Nessie phenomenon was the subsequent actions of a local water bailiff, Alexander Campbell.

In addition to his day job on the loch, Campbell was also an amateur journalist and on hearing of the Mackays' encounter, he promptly interviewed the couple. The resulting article was published in the *Inverness Courier* a few weeks later under the headline 'Strange Spectacle on Loch Ness – What Was It?'

The editors of the national daily newspapers in London's Fleet Street certainly thought they knew when they picked up on Campbell's article early in June 1933: a sure-fire story to send their circulations rocketing. Ever since the release of the original Hollywood blockbuster, *King Kong*, a few months previously, America had been in the grip of monster mania. To the Fleet Street editors, the chance of catching a scoop sighting of a monster in their own backyard – and a real one at that – was just too good to pass up. Journalists were duly dispatched north and were soon reporting back on a rash of sightings of the 'Loch Ness Monster' as it was now officially known. Many of these were unattributed or suspiciously fortunate for the viewer. One, however, by George Spicer and his wife, was deemed particularly newsworthy, as the couple had reported seeing the creature on land, waddling across the lochside road before plunging beneath the water. By the end of 1933, interest in the creature had reached such heights that Bertram Mills Circus had offered the substantial reward of £20,000 for its live capture and huge steel cages had been built on the shore to house it. Moreover, the London *Daily Mail* had engaged the services of the famous big-game hunter Marmaduke Wetherell to deliver the beast to an increasingly

As public interest reached fever pitch during 1933-34, it seemed only a matter of time before the monster was captured. Early Nessie-hunters, seemingly taking their cue from 'King Kong', constructed this huge steel cage, 30 foot long and 25 foot high, on the banks of the loch in 1934, to house the beast.

obsessed public. The plot of *King Kong* was being re-enacted in the Scottish Highlands – only for real! In fact, such was the anticipation that Nessie would soon be caught that the local Member of Parliament asked the Westminster government's most senior official north of the border, the Secretary of State for Scotland, to place the beast under police protection.

In the end, Wetherell's highly publicised searches came to nothing and his reputation suffered when some 'monster' footprints he discovered were revealed to be a hoax (see p.16). If this disappointment had dented the public's enthusiasm, then the reports of the first photographs of the monster sent it soaring again. The first, taken in November 1933 by local man Hugh Gray, certainly seemed to show a dramatic disturbance in the loch but was too blurred to be conclusive. Not so the next to be published, the iconic 'Surgeon's Photo' which caused a sensation when the *Daily Mail* published it as a world exclusive in April 1934. In fact, despite its occasional detractors, Robert Wilson's image of the monster's head and neck was widely regarded as one of the best pieces of evidence of Nessie's existence for next 60 years. The

(see p.16)

THE SURGEON'S PHOTOGRAPH

Over the years, several photographs purporting to show the Loch Ness Monster have been published. For many people however, one picture above all others gave proof that the Loch Ness Monster really did exist: the 'Surgeon's Photo', taken by respected London gynaecologist, Robert Kenneth Wilson. The grainy black-and-white image of the head and neck of the beast rising from the loch caused a sensation when it was first published as a world exclusive in the London Daily Mail on April 21st 1934, less than a year after the possibility of a large monster inhabiting Loch Ness was first splashed across the front pages. Wilson claimed he had been driving on a bird-watching trip to Inverness when he noticed the disturbance in the loch. He had his camera with him in his car and managed to take two photographs before the beast disappeared. Coming from such a respected source, the credibility of the photograph was widely accepted and it became the iconic image of Nessie for the next 50 years. Wilson only gave one public interview about his famous shot, more than 20 years after the event. Interestingly, he was cautious in acknowledging that the photograph actually showed Nessie... perhaps with good reason.

monster was also captured several times on film during the 1930s although remarkably, given the intense public interest in the subject, the cinematographers all seemed curiously reluctant to show anything more than the occasional blurry still from the footage. The whereabouts of most of these films are now unknown.

Inevitably, the initial public furore died down although sightings continued to be reported sporadically during the next couple of decades. Given the remarkable consistency of what everyone claimed to have seen, the image of the monster that emerged was of a large, long-necked creature with one or more humps on a body that resembled the hull of an upturned boat: 'the nearest approach to a dragon or pre-historic animal that I have ever seen in my life', as George Spicer put it describing his encounter. And while sceptics have claimed that several of these sightings have a whiff of locals seeking their 15 minutes of fame, many more were made by reputable individuals with nothing to gain in reporting their contact.

Given this, it was surely only a matter of time before conclusive proof of Nessie's existence would be found.

It wasn't just the press looking to profit from the emerging Nessie story. Bertram Mills Circus, which performed across England, built part of their travelling show around it and even offered a substantial reward for the monster's capture. Here a model of Nessie is paraded through London in December 1933 to promote the circus' Christmas season. It was activity such as this which caused the scientific community to dismiss the possibility of the monster's existence for almost thirty years.

the Hunt Begins in Earnest

The enthusiasm with which the public embraced the prospect of a large unknown creature in Loch Ness was not shared by the scientific community at large. The sensationalism, not to mention the hoaxes, of the early years of the Nessie phenomenon led most scientists to dismiss it as populist wishful thinking and for the next three decades there was no serious investigation of the mounting body of anecdotal and photographic evidence.

By the 1960s, however, the mood was changing and some researchers now believed that the loch and its potential inhabitant(s) merited serious scientific study. This after all was a decade where science and technology was at the forefront of all human advances, giving men new hearts and reaching far into outer space to place men on the moon. Surely the systematic appliance of science to the search for the creature would finally make the loch give up its secrets?

Over the course of the next four decades, a variety of groups, both foreign and domestic, came to Loch Ness and used increasingly sophisticated technologies to search for answers on and below its surface. In addition to systematic coverage of the loch's surface using powerful cameras, extensive use was also made of underwater microphones and sonar devices to peer into its murky depths. The most common of these, the sonar scanner, would emit a pulse of sound waves into the loch and a sensor would pick up

on the returning 'echoes' reflecting off any submerged object or surface; the strength of the echo signal could then be used to calculate the size of the object creating it. In the 1970s and '80s, sonar scanners were often used in conjunction with underwater strobe cameras. It was using equipment such as this that the famous 'flipper' photographs were taken by Dr Robert Rines and his team in 1972 (see p.12). Miniature submarines were also deployed on a number of occasions, but they too were not a great success.

Teams from Cambridge and Birmingham Universities conducted the first, albeit limited, scientific studies of the loch from 1960 to 1962. However, it was not until the formation of the Loch Ness Phenomena Investigation Bureau in 1962 that extensive and sustained studies of the loch began. Set up by the celebrated naturalist and painter, Sir Peter Scott and Conservative MP David James among others, the LNPIB attracted members from all over the world and in 1965 secured the services of the distinguished American biologist, Professor Roy Mackal, as its scientific director.

Initially, the LNPIB concentrated on surface surveillance, establishing its base camp at Achnahannet, a few miles along the shore south of Urquhart Castle. Here, from a viewing platform overhanging the shore, teams of volunteers would scan up and down the loch using powerful film and cine cameras fitted with large telephoto lenses. Mobile observation vans, similarly kitted out, were also used to study the loch from different locations and viewpoints. Unfortunately, none of the photographs that resulted from these surveys actually produced any hard evidence of the monster's existence.

From 1967, the Bureau began working in close collaboration with a number of academic teams who injected a greater degree of scientific rigour and technological expertise to the largely

(see p.12)

Top: *One of Loch Ness' most dedicated researchers, Tim Dinsdale, at work aboard his launch. From 1960 until his death in 1987, Dinsdale led over fifty expeditions in pursuit of Nessie.*
Bottom: *The flotilla of Operation Deepscan in 1987, one of the most famous expeditions on Loch Ness. Each of the small craft was fitted with echo-location equipment and they moved together along the length of the loch to create a 'sonar curtain' which swept the depths for movement.*

THE RINES PHOTOGRAPHS

The appliance of science to the search for Nessie really came into its own in the 1970s. Foremost amongst the scientists who came to the Highlands looking to prove the existence of an unknown species in Loch Ness at this time was Dr Robert Rines, who headed up a team from the US-based Academy of Applied Science. Using a novel combination of sonar transmitters and submerged cameras, Rines hoped to capture the first underwater images of the monster that would prove its existence once and for all. In August 1972, on a joint expedition with the Loch Ness Investigation Bureau, Rines appeared to have hit the jackpot. His celebrated 'flipper' photograph appears to show something that looks like the diamond-shaped fin of some large aquatic creature. Three years later, Rines produced another sensational image of what seemed to be the gnarled head of the monster. Taken together, these images did much to cement the idea in the public's imagination of Nessie as a plesiosaur, particularly when Sir Peter Scott, the celebrated naturalist and painter, pronounced that the Rines' photographs were genuine proof of Nessie's existence. Inevitably perhaps, the truth of the matter was more prosaic: it was revealed that the flipper photograph had been enhanced from its original by unknown persons (possibly magazine staff) while the 'gargoyle' head was subsequently interpreted to be a sunken tree stump.

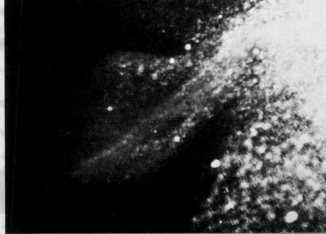

The famous 'flipper' photograph.

volunteer-run body. The following year, a team from the University of Birmingham led by Professor D.G. Tucker installed a prototype sonar device in Urquhart Bay that established an acoustic 'screen' across the breadth of the loch; no object would be able to pass through the sonar beam without being recorded. In a two-week period, several large mobile contacts were made whose size and behaviour defied scientific explanation. In 1969, two other expeditions, an independent survey by the New York Aquarium and a Bureau project involving the submersible *Pisces*, also recorded sonar traces which have failed convincing explanation.

A new era for the scientific exploration of Loch Ness dawned in 1972 with the arrival of Dr Robert Rines from the Academy of Applied Science in New Hampshire. Rines' previous research work at the Massachusetts Institute of Technology had made significant contributions to the field of high-definition sonar scanning and he planned to use this expertise to track down whatever was lurking in Loch Ness. Working in tandem with the LNPIB, the Rines team brought a new sense of purpose to the research, which immediately began to pay dividends. In August 1972, they made a series of major sonar contacts and followed this up with one of the most spectacular and contentious images ever produced at the loch – the so-called 'flipper' photograph.

A number of prominent scientists were quick to back the validity of Rines' results, or at least acknowledge that they were not the product of a hoax. Sir Peter Scott even devised a scientific name for Nessie based on the flipper image, *Nessiteras rhombopteryx* (meaning 'the wonder of Ness with the diamond-shaped fin'), which allowed it to be classified as a protected wildlife species under British law. Together with the gargoyle-head photograph that was captured in 1975, Rines' images caused a sensation when they were first published and were seized upon in the popular press around the world as the definitive proof everyone had been waiting for. Unfortunately, the scientific rigour and indeed the credibility of the Academy's work at Loch Ness was soon brought into question, and in the end, after such high hopes, it was largely discounted by some researchers.

However, the hunt continued. The LNPIB had been wound up in 1972 and its mantle passed to a new team, the Loch Ness Project, under the leadership of naturalist, Adrian Shine. From the 1980s through to the new millennium, the work of the Project was supplemented by various teams from around the world who conducted various underwater searches using increasingly sophisticated

sonar technologies. As with earlier investigations, these investigations produced nothing new or concrete apart from a few unusual contacts.

Webcams are now being deployed at various points around the loch in the hope that their continuous presence will finally record some tangible evidence. For in spite of the huge expenditure of resources over the past 50 years, convincing, unequivocal proof of the monster's existence continues to evade researchers. Perhaps that is the real mystery of Loch Ness.

Some of Dr Robert L Rines' images caused a sensation when they were published in 1970s. This one seemed to confirm anecdotal eyewitness accounts of the Loch Ness Monster as a long-necked creature resembling a plesiosaur.

Anthony 'Doc' Shiels' 1977 photo of the Loch Ness Monster seems to good to be true, and is referred to as the 'muppet photo' by sceptics.

Shadows of Doubt?

Shortly before his death in 1936, the writer G.K. Chesterton commented that 'many men have been hanged on less evidence than there is for the Loch Ness Monster'. As we've seen, since then, a huge body of evidence has accumulated: 1000-plus reported eyewitness accounts, numerous films, countless photographs and several sonar reports that have been difficult to explain by conventional means. However, just how much of this evidence would stand up in court?

Seasoned Nessie hunters now discount many of the reported eyewitness accounts as unreliable. While the Loch Ness Phenomenon Investigation Bureau and its successor, the Loch Ness Project, produced little positive evidence of their own, one of the major achievements of their extensive surveillance programmes was the uncovering of many natural phenomena and optical illusions that they believed accounted for many of the eyewitness accounts. Floating tree trunks, boat wakes and those left by groups of swimming birds, irregular wave patterns, seismic gasses erupting from the Great Glen Fault and animals such as seals, otters and even swimming stags have all been identified or proposed as the true causes behind many of the 'sightings'. The Loch Ness

Project was even able to demonstrate that many of the large sonar contacts that various teams had noted may have been caused by huge underwater waves that sweep the length of the loch, but which are undetectable on the surface.

On the face of it, it seems astonishing that such mundane objects could be confused for something monstrous by so many people. The answer probably lies in the anticipation that everyone brings with them, consciously or not, when visiting Loch Ness. The hold that the Nessie

One of the more recent theories accounting for some early Nessie sightings: swimming elephants. Travelling circuses were known to use the road beside the loch en route to and from Inverness. They may have paused for a rest, and allowed the elephants a relaxing swim.

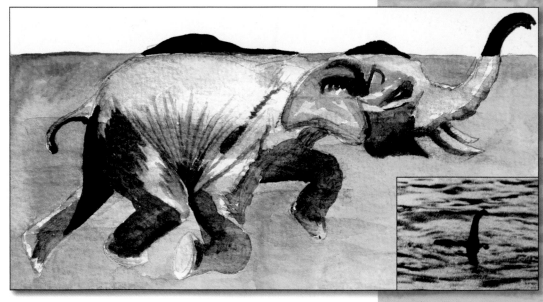

Forestry Commission worker, Lachlan Stuart, took this photo in 1951. He later confessed that the 'humps' were in fact floating bales of hay covered in tarpaulin.

phenomenon has on popular culture is such that we are all preconditioned to expect to see the creature. So, of course, when something not immediately recognisable is spotted on the water… we see what we want to believe.

It seems that even some of the scientists were not immune to seeing what they wanted to see. A closer examination of some of the scientific evidence suggests that flaws in technique and lack of scientific discipline may have resulted in false positive search results. The sonar and photographic

═ FAMOUS HOAXES ═

No sooner had the news first surfaced that something may have been lurking beneath the dark waters of Loch Ness that hoaxers began trying to fool believers and sceptics alike of the monster's existence. The earliest of these, where a local is believed to have used a hippo's foot umbrella stand to mark out 'monster footprints' on the shoreline, occurred in December 1933, just a few months after the story first broke. The prints were quickly exposed as a hoax but not before they had fooled Marmaduke Wetherell, a flamboyant big-game hunter employed by the London *Daily Mail* to track down Nessie. Having been ridiculed and publicly humiliated by the *Mail* as a result, Wetherell plotted his revenge – which resulted in perhaps the best and most enduring Nessie hoax of all. Wetherell and a group of conspirators photographed a toy submarine with a sculpted neck and head floating in the loch, and through the agency of a respected Harley Street doctor sold it to the *Mail* as definitive proof of the monster's existence. This was of course, the iconic 'Surgeon's Photo' (see p.6), and crude as it seems – and was – the world largely believed in it. It was a confession by one of the hoaxers 50 years later that revealed the truth. The scams have continued ever since and have ranged from doctored photographs, fake fossils, and even the planting of a pair of conger eels on the shore. Few of these hoaxes survived any serious scrutiny but taken together with the ongoing disputes about the quality of some of the scientific studies undertaken, they have undermined people's willingness to believe in the possibility of Nessie's existence.

evidence acquired by the Academy of Applied Science for instance, was criticised by some in this respect.

It's also clear that the evidence has been contaminated by the number of hoaxers drawn to the loch over the years. Many of the famous photographs of Nessie, for example, have been shown in fact to have been mischievously concocted on site or else been the product of some subsequent creative retouching. In 1951 Forestry Commission employee Lachlan Stuart snapped a series of mysterious humps rising from the loch, which he subsequently confessed to being tarpaulin-covered hay bales. The famous image of a large shape swimming beneath Urquhart Castle, taken a few years later by bank manager Peter McNab, was subsequently revealed to be a doctored photograph. The suspect images produced during the 1970s and '80s by some Nessie hunters, such as Frank Searle and Anthony Shiels, entertained more people than they convinced and even the iconic 'Surgeon's Photo' was shown to be less than it seemed.

Yet for every hoaxer and every contact explained in terms of the conventional, there are another 100 people who will swear that what they saw in the loch was the genuine article. And there are some sightings that are very difficult to explain away.

Perhaps the most remarkable of these was that made by Father Gregory Brusey, a Benedictine monk at the abbey in Fort Augustus. In the autumn of 1971, Brusey and a friend were walking in the grounds of the monastery, overlooking the loch, when they observed a considerable disturbance in the water some 300 yards out from the shore. 'We saw quite distinctly the neck of the beast standing out of the water to a height of about 10 feet', he recalled. 'It swam towards us at a slight angle, and after about 20 seconds disappeared. It gave us a feeling of something from another world.'

Absence of evidence is not, it would seem, evidence of absence.

Top: *Hugh Gray took what was hailed as possibly the first photographic evidence of the monster in November 1933. It was subsequently believed to be a shot of his dog swimming with a stick in its mouth.*

Bottom: *Frank Searle was one of the more colourful characters involved in the monster searches of the 1970s and '80s. He produced dozens of photographs, like this one of a floating log, which he claimed to be of Nessie. All, however, were deemed fakes.*

Nessie Revealed?

Regardless of how the majority of sightings of Nessie have been accounted for and explained, if we accept none other than Father Brusey's testimony as genuine, then this does clearly point to the existence of a large creature in Loch Ness. And if such a 'monster' really does exist, what on earth could it be?

The popular perception of Nessie, built up since the early days of the phenomenon, is of a long-necked creature with one or more humps along its back, which regularly swims on or close to the surface and which is capable of rising up from the water. The recorded close encounters have been remarkably consistent in describing one or more of these features and the physical characteristics have led to the creature being depicted as some kind of plesiosaur, the large prehistoric marine reptile that roamed the oceans more than 100 million years ago. Given that plesiosaurs are believed to have become extinct some 65 million years ago in the same catastrophe that wiped out the dinosaurs, identifying a living example in Loch Ness would indeed be a remarkable discovery.

However, it wouldn't be the first time such an event had happened. Scientists had also believed that the deep water fish, the coelacanth, had been extinct for about the same amount of time, until that is a living specimen turned up in 1938, with several other examples following. This was a precedent that the most ardent Nessie hunters clung to during the long, uneventful watches from the shore or during the many hours poring over sonar readouts.

Yet for all the plesiosaur's apparent physical similarities with the eyewitness accounts, there is a greater weight of scientific evidence counting against it being considered as a realistic candidate for Nessie. The geology of the region, for example, shows that Loch Ness in its current form only came into being some 10,000 years ago, having been frozen solid for the 20,000 years prior to that during the last Ice Age. If colonies of plesiosaurs had survived beyond their presumed extinction 65 million years ago to then populate the loch, they would be expected to turn up somewhere in the fossil record for the intervening period, which they do not. Also, with an average temperature of just above 5 °C, Loch Ness is too cold for the warm-blooded reptiles to survive and even if by chance they did, the fish stocks in the loch are considered by scientists to be insufficient to support a warm-blooded creature of the reported size. Moreover, a study of plesiosaur fossils has led some commentators to claim that the bone structure of

Opposite:
The Elasmosaurus is a type of plesiosaur which roamed the oceans over 100 million years ago. A study of plesiosaur fossils has led some commentators to claim that the bone structure of its neck could not have supported the creature raising its head clear of the water.

The popular perception of Nessie is of a long-necked creature with one or more humps on its back, similar in appearance to the plesiosaurs.

however, is that any belief in these unknown species is simply not supported by any hard evidence, recorded either at Loch Ness or indeed anywhere else.

A more plausible candidate was put forward in 1993 by the leader of the Loch Ness Project, Adrian Shine. He suggested that many of the hump sightings could be accounted for by the presence of a sturgeon, a large, reptilian-looking fish that has been known to migrate from the sea to spawn in freshwater rivers and lakes. The largest know examples of the species have been measured at over 20 feet in length and estimated to be almost two centuries old. They tend to swim at depth but do occasionally surface and since they only enter freshwater to spawn, visits to Loch Ness would be sporadic, as would be any sightings of them. Countering Shine's proposition is that fact that the varieties of sturgeon that match these characteristics have never been identified anywhere in Britain. However, new species and unusual varieties of known species are regularly discovered and it is not beyond reasonable belief that just such a sturgeon may yet come to light. Remember the coelacanth!

its neck could not have supported the creature raising its head clear of the water, as in the Surgeon's Photo or as Father Brusey described.

Believers like Peter Scott and Roy Mackal countered these points by suggesting that a plesiosaur-type creature could have adapted to the environment in the loch and evolved beyond what existing evidence leads us to deduce about the creature. Similarly, evolved variants of known creatures have also been proposed over the years including giant eels, long-necked newts and seals. The truth,

But while Adrian Shine's sturgeon theory is the most compelling to date and goes some way towards explaining many of the 'hump' sightings, those who witnessed long-necked creatures, such as Father Brusey, still defy conventional explanations. The mystery continues.

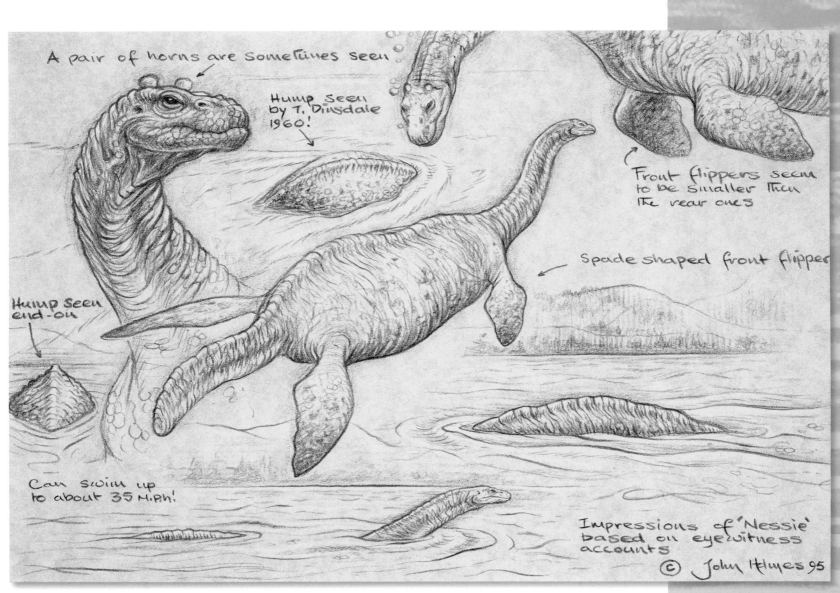

the Last Word?

So, almost eighty years after the story first grabbed the modern world's attention, we still cannot give a definitive answer to the question, 'Does the Loch Ness Monster really exist?' From a human perspective, the evidence for a creature or creatures inhabiting the loch appears overwhelming and compelling and yet, as we have seen, sustained and systematic photographic and sonar surveillance over several decades have been incapable of producing definitive proof.

Could all of the 1,000 or so people who are on record as having seen 'something' in the loch been mistaken or has there been a mass delusion? Certainly, because Nessie is so engrained in popular culture, everyone visiting the loch brings an expectation of the possibility of seeing the monster; given this, it perhaps isn't surprising that those unfamiliar with the loch's subtle moods and of the habits of its regular inhabitants were quick to claim sightings. Interestingly, as we move forward in a new century, reported sightings of Nessie have dropped to just a handful each year (as indeed have UFO sightings); this at a time when mobile phones with cameras have become an essential part of everyday life and always within reach to record an eyewitness account.

But while many of the eyewitness reports can be discounted as the product of exhuberant wishful thinking, there is still that solid core of close contacts that defies explanation within the bounds of the known world. As technology and scientific advancement continues to shrink the world and demystify much of it, it would be nice to think that somewhere in a small corner of the Highlands of Scotland, a creature that has survived for countless generations will continue to evade detection. As Father Brusey told the New York Times several years after his own dramatic experience, 'we ought to leave the monster alone. In this technological age, we've placed a label on everything. I am a champion of the unknown. Mystery intrigues people, and so it should remain.'

DUNCAN
Consulting Specialist and Hairdresser gives advice freely on the delicate matter of Hair Additions. Only the best natural hair used. Phone 42135.
43 SOUTH CLERK STREET, NEWINGTON, EDINBURGH

WEEKLY SCOTSMAN

SMT for VAUXHALL
71 Lothian Road, Edinburgh, 3

SCOTLAND'S INTERNATIONAL WEEKLY

No. 5273 VOL. 101   THURSDAY, JUNE 16, 1960   POSTAGE: 2½ (CANADA, PER MAGAZINE POST, 1d) Price 4d

THE MONSTER SURFACES

VISITING LOCH NESS

If you are visiting Loch Ness and would like more detail about Nessie, then help is at hand. There may only be one monster but there are two monster exhibitions.

Conveniently, The Loch Ness Exhibition Centre and the Original Loch Ness Monster Visitor Centre are both based at Drumnadrochit, a short distance from Urquhart Castle and are well signposted on the main road along the north shore of the loch.

The Loch Ness Exhibition Centre is based around a high-tech multi-media presentation that takes visitors through seven themed areas. Using a highly effective mix of lasers, digital projection and special effects, the exhibition charts the history of the monster by exploring Scotland's geological past, its folklore and the various research projects carried out on the loch. Designed and narrated by Loch Ness Project leader, the naturalist Adrian Shine, the exhibition presents the Nessie phenomenon in the wider context of the loch's scientific and environmental setting. One of its real strengths is its close association with the Loch Ness Project team, which means that many of the displays are built around original research equipment and authentic underwater films.

www.lochness.com/loch-ness-monster-exhibition.htm

The Original Loch Ness Monster Visitor Centre takes a less scientific approach to the Nessie phenomenon, focusing chiefly on the evidence that exists to date of the monster through legend, photographs and film of sightings, and largely delivered via a cinema-style audiovisual show.

www.lochness-centre.com/exhibition.htm

If you would like something a bit closer to the action, there are several companies offering cruises on the loch itself. A couple of these, such as the *Deepscan* operating from the Loch Ness Monster Exhibition Centre or Loch Ness Cruises's *Nessie Hunter* have actually taken part in the various research projects and now ply their way on the loch largely for the benefit of casual visitors, private groups and visiting media teams. They run regular hourly, half day, evenings or full-day-cruises that offer great views of Urquhart Castle and the Great Glen from the best vantage point – the loch!

RECOMMENDED READING & WEBSITES

Nessie – The Legend of The Loch Ness Monster Betty Kirkpatrick, Crombie Jardine 2007. A basic overview of the mystery of the Loch Ness Monster touching all the bases and complete with its own Nessie-spotting diary.

Loch Ness And Inverness Julie Davidson, Colin Baxter 2003. An attractively illustrated guide which explores the mysterious Loch Ness, as well as the city and environs of Inverness.
The Loch Ness Monster: The Evidence Steuart Campbell, Birlinn 1986, 2002. A very scientific, and at times rather clinical, look at the Nessie phenomenon. Ideal for serious sceptics.
The Encyclopaedia of the Loch Ness Monster Paul Harrison, Robert Hale 2000. A reference guide bringing together all the facts and fables surrounding Nessie. Excellent for browsing and dipping into.
The Loch Ness Story Nicholas Witchell, Corgi 1989. In spite of its age, this is still a thorough, balanced and honest account of the history of the investigations from 1933 to the late 1980s, from a respected BBC journalist.
http://en.wikipedia.org/wiki/Loch_Ness_Monster Loch Ness Monster Nessie on Wikipedia. An excellent introduction to the topic.
www.nessie.co.uk The Legend of Nessie. The self-proclaimed 'Ultimate and Official Loch Ness Monster Site' is packed with documented evidence, film, first-hand accounts, stories, scientific studies and expeditions.
www.loch-ness.org Tony Harmsworth's Loch Ness Information Site. A detailed, wide-ranging and personal site covering every aspect of the Loch Ness Monster phenomenon from someone closely involved in the searches during the 1980s and '90s.

Published in Great Britain in 2009 by
Colin Baxter Photography Ltd, Grantown-on-Spey,
Moray PH26 3NA, Scotland
www.colinbaxter.co.uk

Text by James Carney © 2009 Colin Baxter Photography Ltd.

ISBN 978-1-84107-413-9
Printed in China

Photographs © 2009 by:
Colin Baxter: Front cover, pages 2, 3. Dr Neil Clark, University of Glasgow: page 15.
Mary Evans Picture Library: back cover. Victor Habbick Visions/Science Photo Library: page 1.
Emory Kristof/National Geographic/Getty Images: page10.
Fortean Picture Library: Front cover (inset), pages 6, 11 (top), 11 (bottom), 14, 16, 17 (top).
Andreas Meyer/123rf.com: page 18. Mirrorpix: pages 12, 13, 17 (bottom).
The Natural History Museum, London: pages 20, 21.
Newsquest (Herald & Times). Licensor www.scran.ac.uk: page 8.
NmeM Daily Herald Archive/Science & Society: page 9. John Robertson/Alamy: page 22.
Royal Commission on the Ancient & Historical Monuments of Scotland. Licensor www.scran.ac.uk: page 5.
The Scotsman Publications Ltd. Licensor www.scran.ac.uk: page 23.

Front cover: *Loch Ness, and the famous 'Surgeon's Photograph' of 1934.* Page 1: *A modern interpretation of a plesiosaur-like creature, thought to resemble the Loch Ness Monster.* Back cover: *'Nessie' and her offspring.*